Questions in
Standard Grade and Intermediate 1
Physical Education

Malcolm Thorburn

Text © 2005 Malcolm Thorburn
Design & layout © 2005 Leckie & Leckie Ltd.
Cover image © Caleb Rutherford

1st Edition (reprinted 2007)

ISBN-13 978-1-84372-379-0
ISBN 1-84372-379-4

Published by:
Leckie & Leckie,
3rd Floor,
4 Queen Street,
Edinburgh,
EH2 1JE

Tel: 0131 220 6831
Fax: 0131 225 9987

enquiries@leckieandleckie.co.uk
www.leckieandleckie.co.uk

Special thanks to:
BRW (creative packaging), Caleb Rutherford (cover design), Pumpkin House (concept design, page layout and illustration), Roda Morrison (copy-editing) and Tara Watson (proofreading) and Jim Ferguson (content review).

A CIP Catalogue record for this book is available from the British Library.

® Leckie & Leckie is a registered trademark

Leckie & Leckie Ltd is a division of Huveaux plc.

CONTENTS

INTRODUCTION   **4**

Section 1 – ACTIVITIES

Nature and purpose   **5**
    Nature and purpose   5
    Creativity   8
    Tactics   9

Official/Formal and unwritten rules   **11**
    Rules   11
    Conduct and behaviour   13
    Scoring   14

Roles and function   **15**
    Roles and responsibilities   15
    Personal and physical qualities   16

Section 2 – THE BODY

Structure and function   **17**
    Oxygen transport system   17
    Body structure   19
    Joints   20
    Movement of a hinge joint   20

Aspects of fitness 1: Physical fitness   **21**
    Cardiorespiratory endurance   21
    Muscular endurance   23
    Strength   25
    Speed   27
    Power   29
    Flexibility   31
    General physical fitness questions   33

Aspects of fitness 2: Skill-related fitness   **34**
    Co-ordination   34
    Agility   34
    Balance   35
    Reaction time   36

Aspects of fitness 3: Mental fitness   **37**
    Mental fitness   37

Training and its effects   **38**
    Warm up   38
    Warm down   38
    Principles of training   39
    Methods/types of training   40
    Training within activities   40

Section 3 – SKILLS AND TECHNIQUES

Techniques   **41**
    Skills and techniques   41

Ways of developing skill   **44**
    Skill learning   44
    Principles of effective practice and refinement   45
    Feedback   46

Mechanical principles   **48**
    Balance   48
    Transfer of weight   49
    Application of force   50
    Rotation   51
    Resistance   51
    Follow through   51

Section 4 – EVALUATING   52

Section 5 – INTERMEDIATE 1 PHYSICAL EDUCATION   56

Answers to questions   pull-out answer section

Questions in Standard Grade & Intermediate 1 Physical Education is designed to help you prepare for two assessable areas of your course: Knowledge and Understanding and Evaluating.

Knowledge and Understanding

There are three areas within Knowledge and Understanding. These are: 'Activities'; 'The Body'; and 'Skills and Techniques'.

Activities involves you studying the nature and purpose of different categories of activities, the official/formal and unwritten rules which define activities, and various roles and functions within activities.

The Body involves you studying the structure and function of the human body, and different aspects of fitness and training and their effects.

Skills and Techniques involves you studying concepts of skills and techniques, ways of developing a skill and mechanical principles which underpin effective performance.

Ensure that you are familiar with the precise area of knowledge and understanding which questions are asking about. You should be able to attempt most questions. Some questions specifically ask about knowledge and understanding at credit level.

These are highlighted with the following sign

Evaluating

In your course you will evaluate performance by observing and describing sporting actions in different activities, and suggesting improvements. This will involve you recognising basic actions, observing fitness levels and studying in detail different techniques and how they affect the development of quality performance.

Advice on answering questions

Exemplar answers are provided for both knowledge and understanding and evaluating questions. To help you with your revision, we recommend that you obtain a copy of Leckie & Leckie's other Standard Grade Physical Education book, *Standard Grade & Intermediate 1 Physical Education Course Notes*, from your school or bookshop.

At the foot of every page of questions, you will find a page reference to Leckie & Leckie's *Standard Grade & Intermediate 1 Physical Education Course Notes*. Refer to these pages for help in answering the questions.

Leckie×Leckie

STANDARD GRADE & INTERMEDIATE I
Physical Education
course notes

Malcolm Thorburn

See pages 6–16 of Standard Grade & Intermediate 1 Physical Education Course Notes.

Nature and purpose

Key content areas:
- Individual or team activities
- Directly competitive, indirectly competitive and non-competitive
- Objective or subjective scoring systems
- Indoor or outdoor activities
- Reasons for participation in different activities

Important points:
- Some activities can only be performed individually (e.g. squash) or as part of a team (volleyball). Other activities can be performed both on your own and as part of a team (e.g. tennis).
- Different individual and team activities can be directly competitive, indirectly competitive or non-competitive.
- The outcome of different team and individual activities, which are either directly competitive or indirectly competitive, is decided by a variety of objective or subjective scoring methods.
- There are many different reasons why people participate in different activities – social, physical, health and personal.

Individual or team activities

1 Tick the correct boxes in the table below for these different activities.

Activity	Individual activity	Team activity
Volleyball		✓
Social dancing		✓
Marathon running	✓	
4 x 400 m relay		✓
Tennis	✓	✓
1500 m	✓	

Directly competitive, indirectly competitive and non-competitive

2 Explain the major difference between directly and indirectly competitive activities.

Objective or subjective scoring systems

3 Copy and complete the following grid.

Activity	Objective/subjective	How results are decided
Gymnastics	subjective	
Netball		
Cricket	objective	
Table tennis		Number of games won. Each game up to 21 points
Ice dancing		Marks for technical merit and artistic impression
Swimming		

4 Choose one individual activity and one team activity which have objective scoring systems. For each, explain how play is continued in the event of the score being level at the end of the contest/match.

Individual activity:
Explanation:

Team activity:
Explanation:

5 Describe one activity where, in the event of the score ending level (a tie/draw), further participation is not possible and the result has to be decided by other means.

Activity:
Explanation:

6 Choose one activity which uses a subjective scoring system. Describe some of the different criteria which can be used for awarding different marks/points.

Activity:
Explanation:

Indoor or outdoor activities

7 Explain the main reasons why competitive table tennis and badminton games take place indoors.

See page 19 of Standard Grade & Intermediate 1 Physical Education Course Notes.

Reasons for participating in different activities

8   There are many reasons why people participate in activities – reasons can be social, physical, health or personal in nature. Match each of the following descriptions to a different reason for participation:

physical   **social**   **health**   **personal**

'I enjoy getting out and meeting other people. We all take part together and then go out afterwards.'	
'I like the challenge. I need the thrill of competing against myself when I am rock climbing.'	
'Regular exercise is good for me. It is not too difficult, but demanding enough to help me to live a long and healthy life.'	
'Swimming is my favourite sport. The longer events are great for my endurance and the sprint events are great for improving power.'	

9   Copy and complete the table below. Use your experience of different activities in your answer. Your main reasons for participation should include reference to one social, one physical, one health and one personal benefit. An example answer is provided.

Type of activity	Activity chosen	Your main reason for participation
Team, directly competitive	Football	Social – I enjoy being part of a team. We have trained and played together for many years and all get on well together.
Team, directly competitive		
Individual, indirectly competitive		
Team, indirectly competitive		
Individual, non-competitive		

10 Participation levels in activities can be affected by different factors. Age is one factor that affects levels of active participation.

Choose two different activities, one in which you are most likely to participate at a younger age and one in which participation can be lifelong. Explain why age is a factor in each.

Younger age activity:	Explanation:

Lifelong activity:	Explanation:

11 Other factors, such as **money**, **weather**, **facilities** and **disability**, can affect participation levels in certain activities. Choose two of these factors and explain how each is significant in either helping or reducing levels of participation. An example answer is provided.

Activity: Cross-country running	Factor chosen: Money
Explanation: Cross-country running is quite inexpensive. There are many places you can run free of charge. Apart from the cost of correct training shoes, there are few other costs for a recreational runner.	

Activity:	Factor chosen:
Explanation:	

Activity:	Factor chosen:
Explanation:	

See page 20 of Standard Grade & Intermediate 1 Physical Education Course Notes.

Creativity

Key content area:

- Creativity and principles of play

Important points:

- In most activities you need creativity to devise solutions to different problems.
- There are different ways of being creative; some activities have definite targets, e.g. score more goals, while others have more open-ended aims, e.g. improve certain qualities in performance.

12 Choose one activity with an objective scoring system. Describe how you worked creatively with team mates to try to win. An example answer is provided.

Activity: Volleyball
Explanation: Our opponents were finding it straightforward to predict from where our spike attacks were coming. We decided that we could add more variety to our play by asking our setter to vary the set to unsettle the other team.

Activity:
Explanation:

 CREDIT GRADE EXTENSION
Creativity

13 Choose one activity with a subjective scoring system. Describe how you worked creatively to improve the overall quality of your performance. An example answer is provided.

Activity: Gymnastics (floor routine)
Explanation: In my floor routine, I had three different cartwheels. To begin with, they were all at the same speed, leading with my left hand on each one. I decided I could add to the quality of my routine by varying the cartwheels. For a start, I performed one of them leading with the right hand. Then I varied the speed – I made one quite slow, one quite quick from a standing start and one quite quick from a run-up.

Activity:
Explanation:

See pages 21–22 of Standard Grade & Intermediate 1 Physical Education Course Notes.

Tactics

Key content areas:
- Applying tactics
- Personal and physical qualities in tactics
- Effective communication in tactics

Important points:
- The overall aim of a tactic is to play to your individual/team strengths, and to attempt to exploit your opponent's weaknesses.
- Decisions about your tactics are made before, during and after performance.
- Physical qualities (cardiorespiratory, muscular endurance, speed, strength, power, flexibility) and personal qualities (determination, courage and self-confidence) are important when analysing tactics.
- Possessing good verbal and non-verbal communication skills are important when analysing tactics.

Applying tactics

14 Outline one benefit of using a tactic in a game.

15 Choose one team activity. Name one role you had in that activity. Describe a defensive responsibility and an attacking responsibility that went with this role. An example answer is provided.

Activity: Basketball	Role: Guard
Defensive responsibility: I had to make sure I kept my 'opposite number' away from our basket. The closer she came, the more pressure I put her under.	
Attacking responsibility: I had to help set up our attacking plays by passing to different players. I also took some 'outside' shots if I wasn't being marked and other options were not available.	

Activity:	Role:
Defensive responsibility:	
Attacking responsibility:	

Personal and physical qualities in tactics

16 Officials play important roles in many different activities, for example, the referee in rugby union and umpires in cricket. They require certain personal qualities to help them in their role.

Give two personal qualities required by referees or umpires. Explain why each is important. An example answer is provided.

Activity: Hockey	Role: Umpire	Personal quality: Being fair to both sides
Explanation: The umpires have to treat both teams identically. They need to apply the rules of the game in the same way for both teams.		

Activity:	Role:	Personal quality:
Explanation:		

Activity:	Role:	Personal quality:
Explanation:		

See pages 23 to 25 of Standard Grade & Intermediate 1 Physical Education Course Notes.

17 Performers require many different physical qualities for effective performance. For two different activities describe why different physical qualities are required. An example answer is provided.

Activity: Netball	Role: Wing attack	Physical quality: Speed
Explanation: My position in the team is a wing attacker. This requires speed to move quickly between midfield and attack when setting up attacks.		

Activity:	Role:	Physical quality:
Explanation:		

Activity:	Role:	Physical quality:
Explanation:		

Effective communication in tactics

18 Describe one benefit of using effective non-verbal communication in a directly competitive team game.

CREDIT GRADE EXTENSION
Tactics

19 Choose a tactic from a team activity. Explain how the tactic chosen was well suited for both your individual and team strengths. An example answer is provided.

Activity: Badminton (doubles)	Tactic: Playing 'sides' when defending
Description: When defending, I have good court movement. This helps me move forward and back to play different shots. In addition, my partner is of similar ability to me. As a result, we do not have a weak side which our opponents can exploit by hitting to it when the chance arises.	

Activity:	Tactic:
Description:	

See pages 25 to 27 of Standard Grade & Intermediate 1 Physical Education Course Notes.

Key content areas:

- Safety rules
- Official and unwritten rules of fair play
- Specific rules for different types of activities
- Conduct and behaviour
- Adaptation
- Small-sided games

Important points:

- Rules are designed to shape activities and ensure that everyone can participate on an equal basis.
- All activities have official and unofficial rules of fair play.
- Different activities have different specific rules.
- Good conduct and behaviour are part of good sportsmanship.
- Activities can be adapted to suit particular needs.
- Normal activity rules can be adapted in small-sided games.

Rules

Safety rules

20 Choose two different activities. For each, explain how an item of equipment is designed to help you perform safely. An example answer is provided.

Activity: Cross-country running	Equipment: Correct training shoes
Safety feature: Training shoes need to be able to absorb the force of the runner's heel striking the ground on a continuous basis. Training shoes also need to have a good sole grip.	

Activity:	Equipment:
Safety feature:	

Activity:	Equipment:
Safety feature:	

Official and unofficial rules of fair play

21 Give a safety rule, a rule of fair play and an example of good etiquette, each from a different activity. An example answer is provided.

Activity 1: Trampoline	Safety rule: Must have spotters and mat protection in place.
Activity 2: Hockey	Rule of fair play: Keep stick low to ground when passing.
Activity 3: Football	Code of conduct/etiquette: Return the ball to the other team after an injury stoppage.

Activity 1:	Safety rule:
Activity 2:	Rule of fair play:
Activity 3:	Code of conduct/etiquette:

22 Describe the importance of a safety rule, a rule of fair play and an example of good etiquette, all from the same activity. An example answer is provided.

Activity: Rugby Union
Safety rule: Use of feet in a ruck
Explanation: When opposing players are on the ground, you should be careful not to stamp on them as you try to help your team.
Rule of fair play: Safe play in scrums
Explanation: In a scrum, you must try to keep the scrum 'up' and not try to collapse it.
Conduct and behaviour: Shake hands with the other team
Explanation: After the game, you should shake hands as a way of thanking the opposition.

Activity:
Safety rule:
Explanation:
Rule of fair play:
Explanation:
Conduct and behaviour:
Explanation:

See page 29 of Standard Grade & Intermediate 1 Physical Education Course Notes.

Specific rules for different types of activities

23 Explain the rules and procedures which should be followed for a chosen activity. An example answer which covers penalty taking in football is provided.

Rule:	Any foul which would lead to a direct free-kick that is committed by a team inside their own penalty area leads to a penalty. This allows one player a direct shot from the penalty spot (11 metres out) with only the goalkeeper to beat.
Procedure:	The goalkeeper must keep his feet on the goal line until the penalty kick is taken. The other players all stand outside the penalty area and cannot enter the area until the ball has been kicked. The kicker must wait for the referee's signal (blowing a whistle) before taking the kick. The kicker cannot touch the ball a second time until it has been touched by another player. A penalty will be re-taken if: (1) a team mate or the kicker moves into the area before the kick is taken and the penalty is scored; (2) a defender moves into the area before the kick is taken and the penalty is missed, or (3) the goalkeeper moves from his or her goal line before the ball has been kicked.

Rule:	
Procedure:	

Conduct and behaviour

24 Give examples of good sporting behaviour from a chosen activity. An example answer from badminton is provided.

Activity: Badminton	Examples of good sporting behaviour: When playing badminton it is good sportsmanship to: wait until your opponents are ready to receive serve, apologise if any winning shots were deflected by the net, and shake hands with your opponents after the game.

Activity:	Examples of good sporting behaviour:

See pages 30 and 31 of Standard Grade & Intermediate 1 Physical Education Course Notes.

Scoring

(See also questions 3 to 6 on page 6 about 'Objective or subjective scoring systems'.)

Adaptation

25 Describe two advantages of having more attackers than defenders ('numerical superiority') when practising your attacking skills in a team activity.

Advantage 1:
Advantage 2:

26 Choose one activity. Explain four ways you could adapt it. An example answer from volleyball is provided.

Activity: Volleyball		
Full activity	Key Area	Adapted activity
6 v 6	Number of players	4 v 4
Full height	Net height	Lowered to help players
Maximum 3 touches per team	Number of touches	Team allowed more than 3 touches
Ball must not touch ground	Rule change	Ball allowed to touch ground once each possession

Activity:		
Full activity	Key Area	Adapted activity
	Number of players	
	Rule change	

Small-sided games

27 Give two advantages of playing 'small side' team games as opposed to 'full side' team games.

Advantage 1:
Advantage 2:

See pages 32 and 33 of Standard Grade & Intermediate 1 Physical Education Course Notes.

Key content areas:

- Helping other students
- Role of 'opponents' in practice
- Officiating games
- Personal and physical qualities

Important point:

- There are other types of role as well as that of performer. These include helper, team mate, opponent and official.

Roles and responsibilities

Helping other students

28 Copy and complete the table below. Ensure that your answer links Activity, Role and Task description together for each line of the table. One complete example answer is also provided.

Activity	Role	Task description
Tennis	Official	I was a line judge. It was my task to judge whether the ball was 'in' or 'out'.
Badminton	Opponent	
Volleyball	Team mate	
	Official	
Gymnastics		My partner gave me advice on how to perform my handstand correctly, and then supported me.

Role of 'opponents' in practice

29 There are many different roles you carry out when helping a partner in your class. For example, you help by giving advice, by providing opposition in practices and by making sure that they are safe.

Describe two safety factors you have considered while taking part in two different activities. An example answer is provided.

Activity 1: Swimming	Safety factor: Safe swimming in lanes
Explanation: My group ensured that we swam in one direction only. We then walked back to the start point and repeated this 'lane cycle'. This helped make sure that there were no unnecessary collisions between swimmers in our group.	

Activity 1:	Safety factor:
Explanation:	

Officiating games

30 Choose a game and give examples of the officiating decisions you would be required to make. An example answer from tennis umpiring is provided.

Game	Officiating decisions
Tennis umpire:	When umpiring in tennis it was necessary to keep the score and call it out after each point. I also had to watch that there were no other infringements to the rules, for example through players double faulting on serving, foot faulting or touching the net.

Game	Officiating decisions

Personal and physical qualities

31 Choose an individual or team or group activity. For the chosen activity explain the major personal and physical qualities which you required for effective participation within selected strategies. An example answer from badminton is provided.

Activity: Badminton	Role: Mixed doubles player	Personal quality: Determination
Strategy: Initiating early attacks in games		Physical quality: Strength
Explanation: In our team, we were committed to playing to our team strengths. This involved my partner playing low serves or returns, as often as possible, to encourage the opposing team to lift the shuttle. This provided me with the chance to play a strong smash as an attempted winning shot. For this strategy to work my physical quality (strength) was necessary as was our team determination. This was evident by our determination to play to our identified strategy even if there were times when this was not always successful.		

Activity:	Role:	Personal quality:
Strategy:		Physical quality:
Explanation:		

See pages 35 and 36 of Standard Grade & Intermediate 1 Physical Education Course Notes.

Key content areas:

- The benefits of training
- Different levels of oxygen intake during physical activity
- Effects of lactic acid/oxygen debt
- The purpose of the skeleton
- The functions of tendon, cartilage and ligament
- Muscle functions and groups of muscles
- Joints
- Movements of a hinge joint

Important points:

- The main aim of the oxygen transport system is to help you exercise.
- The respiratory and circulatory systems work together to provide muscles with oxygen.
- Regular exercise increases the size of the heart and helps blood flow.
- When it is difficult for your breathing to supply working muscles with oxygen your muscles will become fatigued due to the build up of lactic acid.
- Muscles function by working in pairs or groups.
- Ball and socket and hinge joints are moveable joints.

Oxygen transport system

32 Complete paragraphs (a), (b) and (c) about the benefits of an efficient respiratory and circulatory system. Use the words below each paragraph only once.

(a) **Oxygen transport system**: The main aim of the oxygen transport system is to help you ___3___. As you ___2___ oxygen intake during exercise (by breathing in) you can participate and train in more demanding ways. The lungs, heart, blood and ___4___ all play an important part in the oxygen transport system. The ___1___ and ___5___ systems work together to provide muscles with oxygen. This enables you to exercise.

respiratory	increase	exercise	muscles	circulatory
1	2	3	4	5

(b) **The circulatory system**: The heart (a muscular pump) is at the centre of the circulatory system. The four chambers of the heart are mostly made up of cardiac muscle. By contracting and relaxing the heart muscles can ___2___ blood around the body. The ___5___ of the heart means that blood is pumped around the body in surges which are called the pulse ___1___ of the heart. The ___3___ carry blood away from the body to the vital organs and limbs (oxygenated blood) and ___4___ return blood to the heart (deoxygenated blood).

beat	pump	arteries	veins	contractions
1	2	3	4	5

(c) **The respiratory system** enables air to be inhaled (breathed in). This allows your circulatory system to work effectively. When you breathe in, oxygen enters your ___1___ and is absorbed into your blood. The ___2___ blood allows the cells within your body to use ___4___ to help you exercise. As you exercise a ___3___ product known as carbon dioxide is produced. This is returned to the lungs by your blood as the circulatory system continues and when you ___5___ out the carbon dioxide leaves your body. When you exercise your breathing is controlled automatically by your brain. You do not often have to 'think' about breathing.

lungs	oxygenated	waste	energy	breathe
1	2	3	4	5

The benefits of training

33 Describe three benefits of regular exercise for your heart.

Benefit 1: *Helps your heart to grow*

Benefit 2: *keeps your heart rate down*

Benefit 3: *More blood is pushed around your body with every beat.*

CREDIT GRADE EXTENSION
Oxygen Transport System

Different levels of oxygen intake during physical activity

34 Explain two benefits of completing a breathing test to measure your maximal oxygen uptake during a minute of exercise.

Benefit 1:

Benefit 2:

Effects of lactic acid/oxygen debt

35 Explain two reasons why lactic acid build up has the effect of slowing you down during activity.

Reason 1:

Reason 2:

36 Explain the training advice you would take into account if you were training for a long distance running or swimming race.

See page 39 of Standard Grade & Intermediate 1 Physical Education Course Notes.

Body structure

The purpose of the skeleton

37 Complete the following paragraph about the purposes of the skeleton. Use the words below only once.

1	*2*	*3*	*4*
organs	**movements**	**blood**	**body**

Your skeleton has four major functions: it supports your __*4*__ ; it protects vital __*1*__ (heart, lungs); __*3*__ is produced within longer bones such as the thigh (femur) and it enables __*2*__ to occur.

The functions of tendon, cartilage and ligament

38 Complete the following boxes (a, b and c) about the functions of tendon, cartilage and ligament. Use the words below only once.

1	*2*	*3*
tendon	**cartilage**	**ligaments**

a	Muscles are attached to the bones of the skeleton by a connective tissue known as a __*1*__ .
b	__*2 3*__ join bones to other bones and help provide stability in joints by preventing over-stretching and over-twisting.
c	__*2 3*__ acts a buffer to protect bones.

Muscle function and groups of muscles

39 Study the pictures of the high jumper.

Explain how the jumper's leg muscles work to help her gain height when jumping.

Joints

40 (i) Identify whether each joint circled is
a hinge joint or a ball and socket joint.

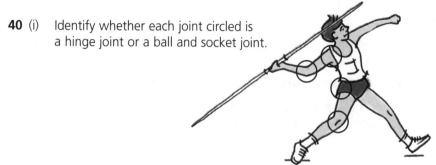

Knee:	Hinge
Hip:	Ball & Socket
Shoulder:	Ball & Socket
Elbow:	Hinge

(ii) Explain the difference between a hinge joint and a ball and socket joint.

 CREDIT GRADE EXTENSION
Joints

41 Study the picture of the runner. Explain how
the muscles, tendons and bones of the main
joint used (the knee joint) work together to
produce efficient movement.

Joint used: Knee joint (Hinge)
Explanation:

Movement of a hinge joint

42 A hinge joint works through an opening and closing (flexing and extending) movement, for
example, when kicking a football. Choose an action within an activity and explain how the hinge
joint works to allow movement. An example answer is provided.

Activity: Basketball Action: set shooting	Explanation: To begin a set shot in basketball the throwing and supporting arms are flexed as are the legs. The ball is close to your forehand so you can sight the basket. As the shot begins you extend your arms and legs. The muscles of the lower legs and arms work with those of the upper legs and arms. This enables the knee and elbow hinge joints to work effectively when carrying out the set shot.
Activity: Action:	Explanation:

See pages 41 and 42 of Standard Grade & Intermediate 1 Physical Education Course Notes.

Cardiorespiratory endurance

Key content areas:

- The effects of cardiorespiratory endurance on performance
- Measuring cardiorespiratory endurance
- Training to improve your cardiorespiratory endurance
- How to calculate your training zone
- Monitoring the effectiveness of cardiorespiratory endurance training
- Monitoring your pulse rate during training
- Training to develop anaerobic endurance

Important points:

- Aerobic exercise involves muscles working with oxygen.
- Anaerobic exercise involves muscles working without oxygen.

The effects of cardiorespiratory endurance on performance

43 Complete the following sentences about the benefits of an efficient cardiorespiratory system. Use the words in bold below. Use each word only once.

oxygen *(1)*   **heart** *(2)*   **blood** *(3)*   **lungs** *(4)*

Your muscles need energy which is supplied by food and ___1___. As you breathe in, air enters your ___4___. There, it is absorbed into your ___3___ and pumped round your body by your ___2___.

44 Choose one activity which requires cardiorespiratory endurance. Describe two benefits of cardiorespiratory endurance on your participation in this activity. An example answer is provided.

Activity: Orienteering
Benefits: The courses for my age and ability last about 60 minutes. Good cardiorespiratory endurance ensures that I can keep running for the whole hour and at a quite fast pace.

Activity:
Benefits:

Measuring cardiorespiratory endurance

45 Describe why any fitness test for measuring cardiorespiratory endurance (for example the Harvard Step Test) should be simple and straightforward to complete.

Training to improve your cardiorespiratory endurance

46 Describe two benefits of regular endurance training for your cardiorespiratory system.

Benefit 1:
Benefit 2:

CREDIT GRADE EXTENSION
Cardiorespiratory Endurance

How to calculate your training zone

47 (i) Explain three considerations which you would take into account to ensure that any cardiorespiratory training you did was beneficial to aerobic endurance rather than anaerobic endurance.

(ii) Explain how you would measure your fitness to ensure your training was effective for developing cardiorespiratory endurance.

Monitoring the effectiveness of cardiorespiratory endurance training

48 Describe a simple method for measuring your pulse rate when monitoring your cardiorespiratory endurance training.

Monitoring your pulse rate during training

49 Explain what is meant by the term 'oxygen debt'.

Training to develop anaerobic endurance

50 Explain a method of training which would work well for developing anaerobic endurance.

See pages 45 and 46 of Standard Grade & Intermediate 1 Physical Education Course Notes.

Muscular endurance

Key content areas:

- The effects of muscular endurance on performance
- Measuring muscular endurance
- Training to improve your muscular endurance
- Monitoring the effectiveness of muscular endurance training
- The effects of increased muscular endurance on the body

Important points:

- Using the same muscle groups repeatedly over long periods of time requires muscular endurance.
- To improve your muscular endurance you need to work muscle groups for long intervals at a relatively low level of intensity.
- Poor muscular endurance leads to fatigue and your muscles will feel tired and heavy.

The effects of muscular endurance on performance

51 Read the four statements below about muscular endurance and select the two which are correct.

- Cyclists need muscular endurance to keep their leg muscles working for a long time.
- Hockey players need muscular endurance to help them shoot.
- When kayaking, my arm muscles need muscular endurance when going upstream.
- On the trampoline, you need muscular endurance to complete a 5-bounce sequence.

Measuring muscular endurance

52 Explain why isolating muscle groups when measuring muscular endurance is necessary.

Training to improve your muscular endurance

53 (i) The most common type of training to improve muscular endurance is circuit training. Write down the major muscle groups which are being exercised at each of the following circuit training exercises.

| Sit-ups | Burpees | Press-ups | Dips | Shuttle run | Step-ups |

Sit-ups:	abdominals	Dips:	triceps
Burpees:	quads	Shuttle run:	groin/calf/hamstring/quad
Press-ups:	latissimusdorsi	Step-ups:	quads

(ii) Choose three of the six exercises shown above. Describe how you could make each exercise increasingly demanding over a number of weeks.

Exercise 1:	
Explanation:	

Exercise 2:	
Explanation:	

Exercise 3:	
Explanation:	

See pages 47 and 48 of Standard Grade & Intermediate 1 Physical Education Course Notes.

Aspects of fitness 1: Physical fitness

 **CREDIT GRADE EXTENSION**
Muscular Endurance

Monitoring the effectiveness of muscular endurance training

54 Circuit training programmes to improve muscular endurance often last many weeks. Give two reasons why regularly re-testing your progress at each exercise station would be useful during your programme.

Reason 1:
Reason 2:

The effects of increased muscular endurance on the body

55 Choose one activity. Explain how muscular endurance could help you sustain performance. An example answer is provided.

Activity: Tennis
Explanation: A tennis match can often last a long time. For this reason it helps if certain muscles groups can work repeatedly for long periods with little rest interval between games. If this can be achieved it helps sustain performance. Leg muscles require endurance to help cover the court throughout the match. Arm and upper body muscles are needed to help play shots throughout the match.

Activity:
Explanation:

See pages 48 and 49 of Standard Grade & Intermediate 1 Physical Education Course Notes.

Strength

Key content areas:
- The effects of strength on performance
- Measuring strength
- Training to improve your strength
- Free-standing weights exercises
- Monitoring the effectiveness of strength training
- The effects of increased strength on the body

Important points:
- The three main types of strength are: static; explosive and dynamic.
- Different activities require different types of strength.
- To improve your strength you need to work muscles groups for short intervals at a relatively high level of intensity.

The effects of strength on performance

56 Read the four statements below about strength and select the two which are correct.
- Swimmers need strength to keep swimming for a long time.
- You need strength in your arms and shoulders to hold a handstand for a few seconds.
- Rugby players need strength to be able to tackle.
- You need strength to putt well in golf.

57 Complete the grid. Explain why different types of strength are required for different activities. An example answer is provided.

Activity	Type of strength required	Explanation
Rugby	Static strength	In various parts of play you need static strength, for example, when remaining static and not allowing your scrum to be pushed backwards involves static strength.
Athletics	Explosive strength	In throwing and jumping events in athletics explosive strength is required. For example, when throwing the javelin maximum energy is used to generate explosive strength.
Gymnastics	Dynamic strength	When performing a floor sequence dynamic strength is required by the major arm and leg muscles to help complete strong flowing movements involving strength.

Activity	Type of strength required	Explanation
Football	Static strength	not being pushed when sheilding the ball
Tenis	Explosive strength	Serving
Rowing	Dynamic strength	being able to pull the oars

Measuring strength

58 Explain why a Standing Long Jump Test would be an effective test for measuring explosive strength.

Training to improve your strength

59 Complete the following sentences using the words in bold below. Use each word only once.

muscle   workload   overload   low

For a strength training programme, you need to exercise specific _____ groups. You need to ensure that the _____ of each exercise is high with _____ repetitions. As the training programme progresses, you need to add _____ to the programme.

Free-standing weights exercises

60 Explain how you could use the same weight machine or free-standing weight exercise for both muscular endurance and strength.

Credit Grade Extension
Strength

Monitoring the effectiveness of strength training

61 These two performers need different types of strength. The gymnast performing a handstand needs **static strength**. For the swimmer, **dynamic strength** is important.

Explain why the gymnast would benefit from isometric exercises and why the swimmer would benefit from isotonic exercises.

The effects of increased strength on the body

62 Improved strength should ensure that you have the capacity to complete actions which require strength and co-ordination, for example, hitting a long pass in hockey. Choose another activity and explain why strength and co-ordination help you complete actions effectively.

See pages 49 to 51 of Standard Grade & Intermediate 1 Physical Education Course Notes.

Speed

Key content areas:

- The effects of speed on performance
- Measuring speed
- Training to improve your speed
- Monitoring the effectiveness of speed training
- The effects of increased speed on the body

Important point:

- To improve speed you need to work muscles groups for short intervals at a relatively high level of intensity.

The effects of speed on performance

63 Choose one individual activity and one team activity. In each, explain how speed is required in one skill. Example answers are provided.

Individual activity: Gymnastics	Skill: Flight (vaulting)
Explanation: The run-up approach requires speed. You need to accelerate quickly over a few steps. You need a fast take-off to help gain flight.	

Team activity: Football	Skill: Dribbling
Explanation: As a winger, I often need speed to pass a defender when dribbling. I knock the ball past him and then sprint after it to regain control.	

Individual activity:	Skill:
Explanation:	

Team activity:	Skill:
Explanation:	

Measuring speed

64 Explain why measuring speed for a hockey player would be more realistic if the test involved changes in direction, for example, when weaving in and around cones as shown below.

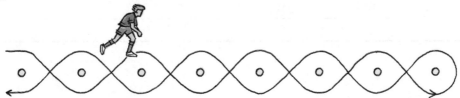

Training to improve your speed

65 Complete the following sentences using the words in bold below. Use each word only once.

        1   2   3   4

anaerobic   strength   muscles   recovery

Speed is best improved by increasing __2__ in the main __3__ required for different activities. When training to improve speed you will be using __1__ (without oxygen) energy most. For this reason you need to ensure that your rest and __4__ time is long enough. This often means that you would work for 1 repetition of an exercise and rest for 4 times as long.

See page 52 of Standard Grade & Intermediate 1 Physical Education Course Notes.

CREDIT GRADE EXTENSION
Speed

Monitoring the effectiveness of speed training

66 Choose one exercise or practice drill that you have used in an activity in your course. Firstly, explain why the exercise or practice drill is specific to the chosen activity. Secondly, explain how you could make the exercise or practice drill progressively more demanding. An example answer is provided.

Activity: Basketball	Speed-related exercise/practice drill: Speed dribble in basketball
Explanation 1: This practice drill is useful to me because it involves me dribbling at the same time as sprinting. I play as a guard; sprinting quickly while dribbling is important in this role.	
Explanation 2: I would add to the difficulty by making the sprint times quicker or by reducing my rest times between the speed dribbles.	

Activity:	Speed-related exercise/practice drill:
Explanation 1:	
Explanation 2:	

The effects of increased speed on the body

67 Improved speed should ensure you have the capacity to complete actions which require speed and agility. Choose an activity and provide an example of where effective speed and agility can together benefit your performance. An example answer is provided.

Activity: Tennis (volleying at net)
Explanation: When moving quickly to the net speed is vital. The quicker you can get to the net the more possible it is to close down your opponent's options for returning shots. When at the net good agility helps you move and react quickly to your opponent's return shot.

Activity:
Explanation:

See page 53 of Standard Grade & Intermediate 1 Physical Education Course Notes.

Power

Key content areas:
- The effects of power on performance
- Measuring power
- Training to improve power
- Monitoring the effectiveness of power training
- The effects of increased power on the body

Important points:
- Power is strength and speed combined.
- Power is very important in explosive events.
- Power can only last for a few seconds.
- To improve your power you need to work muscle groups for short intervals at a high level of intensity.

The effects of power on performance

68 Read the four statements below about power and select the two which are correct.

- Swimmers need power for their racing dive at the start of the race.
- ✗ You need power to dig the ball successfully in volleyball.
- ✗ Hockey goalkeepers need power to help them stop fast shots.
- You need power to throw the discus effectively.

Measuring power

69 Explain why either the Vertical Jump Test or the Standing Long Jump Test are accurate tests for measuring explosive power.

Training to improve power

70 Complete the following sentences using the words in bold below. Use each word only once.

¹ **muscles**   ² **strength**   ³ **weight**   ⁴ **values**   ⁵ **speed**

Explosive power is best improved by increasing __2__ in the main __1__ used for different activities and by completing exercises requiring __5__. If you are using weight training to improve strength, ensure you take into account your own __3__ when calculating training __4__.

 **CREDIT GRADE EXTENSION**
Power

Monitoring the effectiveness of power training

71 Explain how you would monitor the effectiveness of power training.

The effects of increased power on the body

72 Choose one individual activity and one team activity. In each, explain how **power** is required in one skill. Example answers are provided.

Individual activity: Athletics	Skill: Throwing (javelin)
Explanation: To throw the javelin far, you need power. You need to be quite physically strong and have speed in your throwing arm to bring the javelin forward quickly. Linking speed and strength together can produce a powerful throw.	

Team activity: Volleyball	Skill: Spiking
Explanation: To spike effectively in volleyball, you often have to prepare by moving quickly into position to make a strong powerful jump. As you jump, you take your arm back, ready for a powerful downward spike.	

Individual activity:	Skill:
Explanation:	

Team activity:	Skill:
Explanation:	

73 Power is linked to explosive actions that require speed, strength and also split-second timing, for example, a sprint start. Here, the athlete needs sprinting speed as well as a very short reaction time to the starting signal. Choose one skill in one activity where a combination of power and reaction time is required. Explain your choice fully.

Activity:	Skill:
Explanation:	

See page 55 of Standard Grade & Intermediate 1 Physical Education Course Notes.

Flexibility

Key content areas:
- The effects of flexibility on performance
- Measuring flexibility
- Training to improve flexibility
- Monitoring the effectiveness of flexibility training
- The effects of increased flexibility on the body

Important points:
- Flexibility is the range of movement across a joint.
- Having good flexibility reduces the chances of you straining or pulling muscles.
- Controlled stretching exercises can be used to maintain and improve flexibility.

The effects of flexibility on performance

74 Complete the following grid. A completed example answer is provided.

Activity	Static or dynamic flexibility?	Where flexibility is most required
Gymnastics – Headstand	Static	The gymnast requires flexibility in the leg muscles to ensure that the legs are extended with pointed toes.
Swimming		
Hockey		
Rugby		
Athletics		

Measuring flexibility

75 Explain why it is important to extend and stretch carefully and not in a sudden way when measuring flexibility.

See pages 56 and 57 of Standard Grade & Intermediate 1 Physical Education Course Notes.

Training to improve flexibility

76 Complete the following grid.

Exercise	Static or active?	Aim of exercise

CREDIT GRADE EXTENSION
Flexibility

Monitoring the effectiveness of flexibility training

77 Explain how you would monitor the effectiveness of flexibility training.

The effects of increased flexibility on the body

78 Choose one individual activity and one team activity. In each, explain how **flexibility** is required in one skill. Example answers are provided.

Individual activity: Athletics	Skill: Hurdling
Explanation: I needed a big range of movement in my hips to help my performance. I needed a long straight lead leg and a short 'tucked-in' trailing leg. Stretching exercises improved my flexibility for hurdling and allowed me to achieve a good shape when crossing the hurdles.	

Team activity: Dance	Skill: Flight
Explanation: In my dance performance, four of us had to move across the stage doing split leaps in the air at one point. These required flexibility in order to achieve the correct shape in the air with legs straight – one leg out in front and one leg behind – and with arms used for balance.	

Individual activity:	Skill:
Explanation:	

Team activity:	Skill:
Explanation:	

See pages 57–58 of Standard Grade & Intermediate 1 Physical Education Course Notes.

General physical fitness questions

79 Complete the following sentences about when different fitness factors would be required. Use the words in bold below. Use each word only once.

cardiorespiratory endurance   muscular endurance   speed
strength   power   flexibility

To make stretching movements for defending in volleyball, I needed *flexibility*

To be able to throw the javelin far, I needed *power*.

To rebound continuously during the whole game, I needed *muscular endurance*.

To make short fast runs into the penalty area, I needed *speed*.

To keep going for the full 90 minutes, I needed *cardio respiritory enderance*

To hold a handstand, I needed *strength*

80 Complete the following sentences about why different players in a hockey team require different types of fitness. Use the words in bold below. Use each word only once.

cardiorespiratory endurance   muscular endurance   speed   strength
power   flexibility

The midfield players in our team needed ____1____ as they had to do so much running in the game. In defence, the defenders needed ____3____ to cover for each other against attacking players. In attack, our attackers needed ____4____ to keep possession of the ball when under pressure from defenders challenging them. They also needed ____5____ when shooting. The goalkeeper needed ____6____ when diving to save shots. All players needed some ____2____ ____2____ in their arm and leg muscles.

Aspects of fitness 2: Skill-related fitness

Key content areas:

- Co-ordination
- Agility
- Balance
- Reaction time

Important points:

- Co-ordination is the ability to control movements smoothly and fluently.
- Agility is the ability to move the body quickly and precisely.
- Balance is the ability to retain the centre of gravity over your base of support.
- Reaction time is the time taken between the recognition of a signal and the start of the movement.

Co-ordination

81 Complete the following sentences using the words in bold below. Use each word only once.

fluently   **jerkiness**   **sequence**   **complex**   **phase**   **smoothly**

Co-ordination is the ability to control movements ___1___ and ___6___. To perform in a co-ordinated way, groups of muscles work in a specific ___3___ to create effective movements. For difficult skills with ___4___ co-ordination requirements specific practices are required. A triple jumper in athletics practises carrying speed through to the final jump ___5___. This requires co-ordinated body movements in each phase of the jump. Effective co-ordination should ensure that there is no ___2___ when performing a triple jump.

CREDIT GRADE EXTENSION
Co-ordination

82 Choose one individual activity. Explain how co-ordinated movements will help your performance. An example answer is provided.

Individual activity: Swimming (Breast stroke)
Explanation: In this stroke, it is important to establish a pull-breathe-kick action that is co-ordinated and fluent. This helps the timing involved in the stroke and helps you use your leg and arm muscles effectively.

Individual activity:
Explanation:

Agility

83 Explain how agility will help the hockey player complete effectively the dribbling practice in hockey.

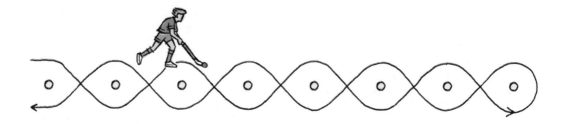

See pages 59 and 60 of Standard Grade & Intermediate 1 Physical Education Course Notes.

CREDIT GRADE EXTENSION
Agility

84 Agility combines elements of flexibility and speed with precision and control. Describe, in detail, one action which combines these physical and skill-related fitness factors. An example answer is provided.

Activity: Athletics (Hurdling)
Flexibility: You need flexibility in the hips to allow you to lean forward with your upper body and for your trailing leg to cross the hurdle. You also need leg flexibility to keep your lead leg as extended as possible as it crosses the hurdle.
Speed: Hurdle races are sprint events. Speed is vital as quickest time determines the winner. Speed is required at the start. A quick pick-up can help you get to the first hurdle first, often a considerable advantage.
Precision: The stride pattern in hurdle races requires precision. Usually in a short sprint you try to take the same number of strides between hurdles. It is vital therefore that you arrive at the first hurdle leading with your favoured leg. This will help ensure your hurdle action is smooth, regular and precise.
Control: In hurdle races you need to keep your body in control. So, if you 'hit' a hurdle with your lead leg, you should try to regain control as quickly and smoothly as possible, so that you lose as little time as possible.

Activity:
Flexibility:
Speed:
Precision:
Control:

Balance

85 Static balances require you to hold a balance, while dynamic balances require you to maintain balance under constantly changing conditions. Complete the following grid.

Balance	Static or dynamic?	Aim of balance

See pages 60 and 61 of Standard Grade & Intermediate 1 Physical Education Course Notes.

CREDIT GRADE EXTENSION
Balance

86 Explain one action where large body movements are required at the beginning of a balance and fine (small) body movements are required to complete the balance. An example answer is provided.

Activity: Volleyball (setting)
Explanation: It is vital when setting to get into position quickly. This involves moving with your whole body in balance so that you are in a low stable balanced position when the ball gently rests in your hands for a split second. After this fine control of the arms and fingers are required as you carefully play the set shot to the position and player required.

Activity:
Explanation:

Reaction time

87 For one individual and one team activity provide an example of when a quick reaction time is useful for effective performance.

Individual activity:
Example:

Team activity:
Example:

Credit Grade Extension
Reaction time

88 In different activities you are required to react to different types of signal. Complete the following grid. Example answers are provided.

Whistle	Netball	In netball the major starts and restarts within the game are signalled by the umpire's whistle. Reacting quickly to such signals is an advantage for retaining or securing possession.
Whistle		
Visual signal	Football	When in possession of the ball you can react and make passing decisions based on the visual signals received from team mates. Such players can indicate where they wish you to play the ball to, without the other team's players seeing the signal.
Visual signal		

See pages 61 and 62 of Standard Grade & Intermediate 1 Physical Education Course Notes.

Key content area:

- Mental fitness

Important point:

- Mental preparation is based on concentration, confidence and motivation.

Mental fitness

89 Explain why mental preparation (thinking ahead) would be an advantage when performing an activity which is physically demanding for a long period.

CREDIT GRADE EXTENSION
Mental fitness

90 Choose one activity. Explain how you would mentally rehearse for participation in the chosen activity. An example answer is provided.

Activity: Badminton
Explanation: When waiting to serve there is an opportunity to take a few seconds to control your emotions and reflect on how the game is going. During this time you can rehearse what your next moves are as you have some time to control the pace of the game. You can decide on which serve might be best bearing in mind your performance strengths and weaknesses and the score within the game.

Activity:
Explanation:

Key content areas:

- Warm up
- Warm down
- Principles of training
- Methods/types of training
- Training within activities

Important points:

- The aim of a warm up is to gradually prepare your body for action.
- The purpose of the warm down is to help your body recover after exercise.
- For a physical fitness training programme to be effective you need to apply the training principles of specificity and progressive overload to your programme. This can be achieved by adapting duration, intensity and frequency in your programme.
- For training to be effective principles of training need to link to chosen methods of training.
- You can train through participating in activities or train outside of activities.

Warm up

91 Complete the following sentences using the words in bold below. Use each word only once.

pulse _(1)_   **stretching** _(2)_   **skills** _(3)_   **jogging** _(4)_   **preparation** _(5)_

A warm up is an important part of your ___5___ for activity. It should begin with some gentle ___4___ to raise your ___1___. After this, you should do some ___2___ exercises that will help your flexibility. You may then want to practise some of the ___3___ involved in the activity.

92 Choose one activity. Explain how you would organise your warm up for this activity. Your answer should include details of two specific exercises you used. An example answer is provided.

Activity: Badminton
Explanation: My warm up consisted of gentle jogging and stretching exercises. I tried to keep both specific to badminton. For my jogging, I moved at a gentle pace around the badminton court – this involved changing direction. For my stretching exercises, I concentrated on the shoulders and trunk. One exercise was called 'trunk twists' and involved turning and twisting from 'face on' to 'side on'. Another was called 'side leans' – this involved using one hand to pull the opposite arm over my head while leaning to the side. I completed each exercise six times as part of my overall stretching.

Activity:
Explanation:

Warm down

93 Warming up before activity and warming down after activity are good ideas.
   (i)   Why is light jogging carried out at the beginning of a warm down?
   (ii) Why is it followed by stretching?
   (iii) Why is a warm down carried out at the end of an activity?

   Give two reasons in each answer.

See page 64 of Standard Grade & Intermediate 1 Physical Education Course Notes.

Principles of training

94 Complete the following table using the words in bold below. Use each word only once.

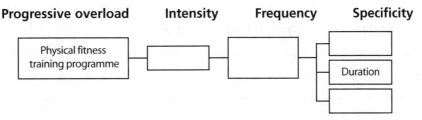

Progressive overload   Intensity   Frequency   Specificity

95 (i) Outline two benefits of assessing your level of fitness at the beginning of a fitness training programme.

   (ii) As your fitness training programme continues, 'overload' is needed. How would you add overload to your programme?

96 Complete the following sentences using the words in bold below. Use each word only once.

   intensive   aerobic   demands   anaerobic   duration

Duration refers to the length of planned time spent training. The _____ of your training varies according to the _____ of the activity. Within the context of a training programme short, _____ training sessions promote _____ fitness improvement; longer, moderately intensive sessions develop _____ endurance.

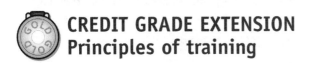 **CREDIT GRADE EXTENSION**
Principles of training

The dangers of over training

97 Explain how over training could be avoided.

Setting intensity levels for different exercises

98 Effective training requires you to work at the correct level of intensity. Complete the following grid. An example answer is provided.

Athlete	Aspect of fitness	Percentage effort (Intensity)	Training session
Long distance runner	Cardiorespiratory endurance	50–60%	Longer, more continuous work with some short rests
	Speed		Shorter, with periods of very hard work and some quite long rests to recover

99 Explain the benefits of lactate tolerance training.

Reversibility

100 Explain why the period of reversibility is short if you have trained for a short period of time and long if you have trained for a longer period of time.

Methods/types of training

Physical fitness training methods

101 Choose two of the following exercises that are often included in general circuit training.

      shuttle run   **squat thrusts**   **press-ups**   **bench jumps**

For each exercise, explain how you could make the exercise progressively more demanding.

Exercise 1:
Explanation:

Exercise 2:
Explanation:

Interval fitness training

102 Some of the most important benefits of interval fitness training are listed below. Complete the sentences. Use each word only once.

      1   *2*   *3*   *4*   *5*
      fatigue   **intensity**   **anaerobic**   **overload**   **aerobic**

It enables high ___*2*___ training to be undertaken. Such training links to periods of rest to avoid ___*1*___ occurring.

It has the capacity to be useful for both ___*5*___ and ___*3*___ purposes.

Progressive ___*4*___ can be carefully added to your training.

103 Complete the grid for both an individual activity and a team activity of your choice. An example answer is provided.

	Activity	Aspect of fitness	Method of training	Fitness test
Individual activity	Gymnastics	Active stretching	Flexibility	Sit-and-reach test
Individual activity				
Team activity				

For each activity, explain why the method of training is effective for the activity and aspect of fitness chosen.

For each activity, explain why the fitness test is effective for the activity and aspect of fitness chosen.

Training within activities

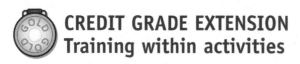

CREDIT GRADE EXTENSION
Training within activities

104 Describe two advantages of a conditioning approach to training.

See pages 68 to 72 of Standard Grade & Intermediate 1 Physical Education Course Notes.

Key content areas:
- Effects of skills and techniques on performance
- Preparation/Action/Recovery
- Overcoming problems in skill learning
- Skill learning environments

Important points:
- A skill describes the purpose of linked sequences of movement. Technique describes the ways of completing a skill.
- Skills and techniques vary in difficulty according to their requirements, your ability and your previous experience.
- Skills should be carried out with maximum efficiency and performed with the minimum of effort.
- You can analyse technique effectively by establishing performance criteria and comparing yourself against a model performer.
- High quality practice for a short time is better than long periods of repeating the same practice.

Skills and techniques

Effects of skills and techniques on performance

105 Complete the following sentences using the words in bold below. Use each word only once.

        1   2   3   4   5

        difficult   **easy**   **complex**   **tiring**   **movements**

When learning to perform a new skill or technique, you try to make it as ___2___ as possible. You can do this by making the ___5___ flow together in a simple order. As you become better, you can make the skill or technique more ___3___. You can make your skill or technique practice more ___1___ in many ways, for example, by practising for longer. This may make it more ___4___ for you.

Preparation/action/recovery

106 For a vault in gymnastics, arrange the following words in the correct order in terms of preparation/action/recovery.

second flight   *2* take-off   *5* landing   *3* first flight   *1* run-up

4

107 Complete the following table, giving two examples of preparation, action and recovery for each skill/technique shown.

Activity	Gymnastics	Badminton	Basketball
Skill/technique	Forward roll	High serve	Jump shot
Preparation 1			
Preparation 2			
Action 1			
Action 2			
Recovery 1			
Recovery 2			

108 Choose one activity. Explain how you could organise practices for the preparation, action or recovery part of a chosen skill or technique. An example answer is provided.

Activity: Squash	Skill/technique: Forehand return of serve

Explanation: I isolated the preparation part of this technique. I completed movement practices that involved me moving quickly from the 'T' to the corner. When doing this, I had to concentrate on moving and turning my shoulders so that my racket would be correctly aligned for the action part of my forehand return of serve.

Activity:	Skill/technique:
Explanation:	

109 Choose a skill or technique from both an individual activity and a team activity. Explain how you organise your practices for either the preparation, the action or the recovery part of the skill or technique. An example answer is provided.

Team activity: Basketball	Skill/technique: Shooting (right-hand lay-up)	P/A/R Area: Action

Explanation: I was driving to the basket well but not scoring enough. I decided to slow down and work on the action part of the technique. I took a step then a jump off my left foot. I took my right arm up high and concentrated on laying the ball softly onto the 'magic spot' of the backboard. The high jump and soft release of the ball helped me score more baskets in practice and then in full games.

Team activity:	Skill/technique:	P/A/R Area:
Explanation:		

Individual activity:	Skill/technique:	P/A/R Area:
Explanation:		

Overcoming problems in skill learning

110 Give two advantages of comparing yourself against a model performer to help overcome skill learning problems.

See pages 76–78 of Standard Grade & Intermediate 1 Physical Education Course Notes.

Skill learning environments

111 Choose two individual activities. For each, describe one way in which the skill or technique practice was made more demanding. An example answer is provided.

Activity: Gymnastics – handstand
Explanation: In the first practice, my partner stood in front of me and supported me with both arms. In the second practice, my partner stood beside me and supported me with one arm only.

Activity 1:
Explanation:

Activity 2:
Explanation:

112 Choose **two** team activities. For each, describe one way in which the skill or technique practice was made more demanding. An example answer is provided.

Activity: Volleyball
Explanation: In a dig practice, the speed of the 'feed' was increased. This meant I had less time to react to the ball coming towards me.

Activity 1:
Explanation:

Activity 2:
Explanation:

113 Number this list of practices from '1' to '4' in order of difficulty, using '1' for the easiest and '4' for the most difficult practice.

Activity: Swimming	
Technique: Back crawl	
Push off from the side, gentle continuous leg kick, take six arm strokes, then stand.	
Push off from the side, hold one float under each arm, leg kick for one width.	
Push off from the side, swim continuously for one 20 m length of back crawl, full stroke.	
Push off from the side, hold one float across chest, leg kick for one length of the pool.	

 CREDIT GRADE EXTENSION
Skills and techniques

114 Give three reasons why learning skills for attacking can often be made easier by having more attackers than defenders in a team game.

Reason 1:
Reason 2:
Reason 3:

Key content areas:

- Safe practice
- Practice methods
- Stages of learning
- Work-to-rest ratio
- Practising under pressure
- Feedback
- Co-operation

Important points:

- The main practice methods are gradual build-up, whole-part-whole, whole and passive/active practices.
- There are three important stages in skill learning: the planning, practice and automatic stages.
- By setting clear training objectives and practising under pressure, you are likely to avoid boredom and your practice will be most effective.
- Feedback is information you receive about your performance.

Skill learning

Safe practice

115 Explain the link between safe practice and your level of ability.

Practice methods

116 (i) Give one reason why repeating a practice can help you learn.

(ii) Give two reasons why practising for too long can be a problem.

117 In this practice, four 'attackers' are trying to keep possession of the ball while staying in the box. There is one 'defender' (wearing a dark top) who has been asked to provide passive opposition.

Explain three ways in which this practice could be made more demanding.

118 Explain why gradual build-up may be a better practice method than the whole-part-whole method for continuous skills or techniques.

 **CREDIT GRADE EXTENSION**
Skill learning

Stages of learning

119 Describe two advantages of being able to carry out some skills or techniques automatically in fast-moving continuous team games.

See pages 81 to 86 of Standard Grade & Intermediate 1 Physical Education Course Notes.

Principles of effective practice and refinement

120 Choose one directly competitive activity. Explain the importance of playing area, level of opposition and number of opponents in helping you to break down the skills of the activity chosen. You should use a different skill for each part of your answer. An example answer for 'playing area' is provided.

Activity: Hockey	
Importance of Playing Area	
Skill: Passing	Explanation: The playing area was made bigger in order to make the skill easier to learn. We had more time to improve the skill – we controlled the ball, looked around, and then passed accurately as we had more space around us.

Activity:	
Importance of Playing Area	
Skill:	Explanation:
Importance of Level of Opposition	
Skill:	Explanation:
Importance of Number of Opponents	
Skill:	Explanation:

121 Complete the following sentences using the words in bold below. Use each word only once.

fatigued   boredom   varied   effective

A principle of _____ practice is that you train for a suitable training time. Too short and improvements will be limited. Too long and you may become _____ and prone to picking up an injury. Training for too long a time can also lead to _____ and a gradual reduction in the amount of progress you make. Having _____ practices is one effective way of reducing boredom.

Work-to-rest ratio

122 Complete the following short sentences using the words in bold below. Use each word only once.

experience   physical   difficulty   practical

The work-to-rest ratio takes into account:

- your previous _____ in an activity
- your level of _____ ability
- the _____ of the skill involved
- the _____ demands involved in the practice.

CREDIT GRADE EXTENSION
Principles of effective practice and refinement

Practising under pressure

123 Practising under pressure often involves adapting and changing the demands of practice in order to make sure practice reflects the demands of competitive performance.

(i) Choose one activity in which you have had to **adapt** a skill or technique in order to improve your overall performance. An example answer is provided.

Activity: Volleyball	Skill/technique: Spiking
Explanation: During a game, many of my diagonal spikes were being retrieved by the opposing team. I adapted the angle of the spike – I began spiking 'down the line'. Having two options made me more successful.	

Activity:	Skill/technique:
Explanation:	

(ii) Choose one activity in which you have had to change a skill or technique in order to improve your overall performance. An example answer is provided.

Activity: Hockey	Skill/technique: Hitting
Explanation: When playing outdoor hockey, I was doing a type of 'slap hit' – my right hand was halfway down the stick. However, this type of hit was often intercepted as it lacked power. I therefore changed my hand position to both hands at the top of the stick. I was able to gain more power in each hit from a larger swing.	

Activity:	Skill/technique:
Explanation:	

Feedback

124 Answer true or false to the following statements on feedback and its importance in your learning:

- Receiving feedback immediately after your performance is best.
- Negative feedback about what you are doing wrong will help you learn.
- Knowledge of results is a useful form of external feedback.
- Detailed feedback on at least 10 different points is needed to learn simple skills.
- Positive feedback on a few key points works well.
- You receive internal feedback during your performance.

See pages 88 to 90 of *Standard Grade & Intermediate 1 Physical Education Course Notes.*

125 This coach is giving feedback. Describe three important points the coach should consider before offering feedback.

126 Explain the difference between internal and external feedback.

127 Explain how one type of internal feedback and one type of external feedback played a part in your performance development. An example answer is provided.

Activity: Orienteering	
Internal feedback: Pace judgement	External feedback: Reading map carefully
Explanation: When I was running, I could usually tell that I was moving at the right pace by using my personal experience of similar Orienteering courses. My past experience let me know how I should feel after a few miles of running in difficult terrain. At the same time, I gained external feedback from being able to read the map carefully. I was able to judge the correct speed to run based on the length of the course and the type of terrain over which I would be moving between the different control points.	

Activity:
Internal feedback:
Explanation:
External feedback:
Explanation:

Co-operation

128 Describe three advantages of co-operating effectively with a partner when practising to improve skills and techniques.

See pages 89 to 91 of Standard Grade & Intermediate 1 Physical Education Course Notes.

Key content areas:

- Balance
- Transfer of weight
- Application of force
- Rotation
- Resistance
- Follow through

Important points:

- Balance is the ability to retain your centre of gravity over your base of support.
- Being in balance helps you transfer your weight when performing different skills and techniques.
- When performing different skills and techniques forces are applied and resisted.
- Follow through is important in kicking, striking and throwing actions.

Balance

129 Study the two figures. One has a static centre of gravity and one has a dynamic (constantly moving) centre of gravity. Identify which is which and explain the reasons for your choice.

130 Choose one skill or technique that requires static balance. Explain three practices of increasing difficulty you completed to improve this skill or technique. An example answer is provided.

Skill/technique: Handstand
Practice 1: I did a handstand against a wall. This provided a lot of support.
Practice 2: I did a handstand with support from my partner. He stood in front of me and provided support with both arms. This provided less support than a wall, but he still had a good hold of me if necessary.
Practice 3: This time my partner stood by my side and provided a single arm support behind my knees. This provided less support than practice 2 – it was more 'up to me' to find my balance. If I lost my balance and began to fall forward, my partner could provide support.

Skill/technique:
Practice 1:
Practice 2:
Practice 3:

See pages 92 to 93 of Standard Grade & Intermediate 1 Physical Education Course Notes.

131 Choose two different skills or techniques, one requiring good static balance and one requiring good dynamic balance. How did you manage to remain still and in control of your centre of gravity in the static balance? How did you manage to remain in control of your centre of gravity in the dynamic balance? Example answers are provided.

Skill/technique requiring static balance: Arabesque in gymnastics
Explanation: To remain still in this static balance, I had to control all my movements as I moved into and out of the balance and, most importantly, during the balance. I started from a standing position and slowly went into the balance and found the best position to hold. When there, I held the balance as still as possible, making some slight adjustments to the positions of my hands and feet. I came out of the balance in a slow, controlled way.

Skill/technique requiring dynamic balance: Spiking in volleyball
Explanation: To remain in control during my spike action, I made sure that I controlled my forward approach to the net. I made sure I jumped up high off two feet. To help me do this, I moved into a balanced jumping position with a quite wide base of support and low centre of gravity. This gave me control when jumping.

Skill/technique requiring static balance:
Explanation:

Skill/technique requiring dynamic balance:
Explanation:

Transfer of weight

132 Complete the following sentences using the words in bold below. Use each word only once.

power   gravity   resistance   distance   height   force

A swimmer uses _____ to overcome _____. A rugby union player taking a penalty kick from a long _____ has a long follow-through in her kick. This helps add _____ to the kick. A long distance runner keeps his centre of _____ at the same _____ as he runs forward.

133 Many actions in different activities involve a transfer of weight from back foot to front foot. For three different activities, choose one skill or technique which is made more effective by transferring weight in this way. An example answer is provided.

Activity: Badminton	Skill/technique: High serve
Explanation: As the racket begins its downswing, you begin to transfer your weight forward. This makes it easier to generate the timing and power needed to serve high and deep to the back of the court.	

Activity:	Skill/technique:
Explanation:	

Activity:	Skill/technique:
Explanation:	

Activity:	Skill/technique:
Explanation:	

134 Choose one activity and explain how improving your transfer of weight has improved your performance. An example answer is provided.

Activity: Indoor hockey	Skill/technique: Push passing
Explanation: I found that by transferring my weight forward from a low angle, placing my left foot close to the ball, I was able to generate more power in my push pass.	

Activity:	Skill/technique:
Explanation:	

Application of force

135 Choose two activities. For the first explain how a short lever is useful for applying force. For the second activity explain how a long lever is useful for applying force. Example answers are provided.

Effective use of short lever
Activity 1: Table tennis
Explanation: Table tennis is a very fast game. You need quick movements and accurate shots. You need to react quickly. You can gain greater control through a short swing and through being quite close to the ball.

Effective use of long lever
Activity 2: Tennis
Explanation: You often need to create power in tennis – for example, when serving and smashing. This is best achieved by a large swing with a straight arm to create a long lever.

Effective use of short lever
Activity 1:
Explanation:

Effective use of long lever
Activity 2:
Explanation:

See pages 94 and 95 of Standard Grade & Intermediate 1 Physical Education Course Notes.

Rotation

136 Describe one technique where rotation is used to enhance performance.

Resistance

137 Choose one activity. Explain how you tried to be streamlined in order to help your performance. An example answer is provided.

Activity: Cycling
Explanation: I wore special tight-fitting clothes and sat in a 'tucked forward' position in order to stay streamlined and reduce drag.

Activity:
Explanation:

138 (i) Give two examples from two different activities of where you used force to overcome resistance. An example answer is provided.

Activity: Swimming
Example of using force to overcome resistance: I used the propulsion from my arm and leg actions to overcome the resistance of the water.

Activity 1:
Example of using force to overcome resistance:

Activity 2:
Example of using force to overcome resistance:

(ii) Give two examples from two different activities of where you used resistance to help create force. An example answer is provided.

Activity: Athletics
Example of using resistance to help create force: I used the resistance from the blocks to create force to help me 'sprint start'.

Activity 1:
Example of using resistance to help create force:

Activity 2:
Example of using resistance to help create force:

Follow through

139 Describe one technique where an effective follow through enhances performance.

See pages 96 to 98 *of Standard Grade & Intermediate 1 Physical Education Course Notes.*

4 EVALUATING

140 Describe the following actions using preparation/action/recovery. An example answer is provided.*

Volleyball – volley

Preparation: Move quickly under ball in balance, adopt steady position with arms and legs relaxed and flexed, eyes watching ball closely.
Action: Play ball in front of forehead with forward and upward stretching movements. Smooth extension of arms and legs as ball is played.
Recovery: Lower arms after volley, resume flexed balanced body position.

(i) Gymnastics – forward roll

Preparation:
Action:
Recovery:

* Please note that in your examination, you will be shown a video of a performance. You are required to suggest improvements as well as observe and describe actions.

Sees page 100 to 101 of Standard Grade & Intermediate 1 Physical Education Course Notes.

(ii) Basketball – left handed lay-up

| Preparation: |
| Action: |
| Recovery: |

(iii) Tennis – backhand

| Preparation: |
| Action: |
| Recovery: |

(iv) Gymnastics – handspring

Preparation:	
Action:	
Recovery:	

(v) Gymnastics – neck spring

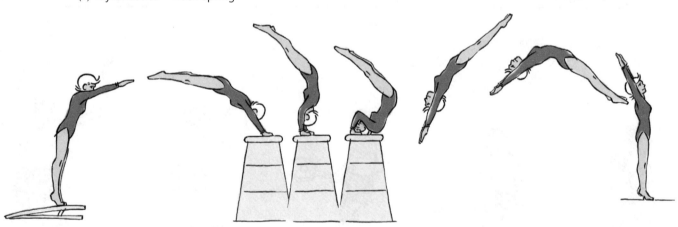

Preparation:	
Action:	
Recovery:	

See pages 100 to 101 of Standard Grade & Intermediate 1 Physical Education Course Notes.

141 As part of your preparation for your evaluating examination observe and describe in as greater detail as possible the following actions using the headings preparation/action/recovery as a guide to your answers. Discuss your answer with your class mates and teacher.

See pages 100 to 101 of Standard Grade & Intermediate 1 Physical Education Course Notes.

PERFORMANCE APPRECIATION (AREA 1)

is a **general** broad view of performance which relates to the three other specific areas of analysis of performance areas. The key concepts in this area are:

The overall nature and demands of quality performance	11 – 13
Technical, physical, personal and special qualities of performance	16
Mental factors influencing performance	37
The use of appropriate models of performance	42
Planning and managing personal performance improvement	44 – 47

PREPARATION OF THE BODY (AREA 2)

is a **specific** analysis of the fitness and training requirements necessary for your performance. The key concepts in this area are:

Fitness assessment in relation to personal performance and the demands of activities	17 – 40
Application of different types of fitness in the development of activity specific performance	40
Physical, skill-related and mental types of fitness	21 – 40
Principles and methods of training	38 – 40
Planning, implementing and monitoring training	40

SKILLS AND TECHNIQUES (AREA 3)

is a **specific** analysis of your skills and techniques needs in performance. The key concepts in this area are:

The concept of skill and skilled performance	41 – 44
Skill/technique improvement through mechanical analysis or movement analysis or consideration of quality	48 – 51
The development of skill and the refinement of technique	44 – 47

STRUCTURES, STRATEGIES AND COMPOSITION (AREA 4)

is a **specific** analysis of the influence of shape, form and design on your performance. The key concepts in this area are:

The structures, strategies and/or compositional elements that are fundamental to activities	5 – 10
Identification of strengths and weaknesses in performance in terms of: roles and relationships, formations, tactical or design elements, choreography and composition	15 – 16
Information processing, problem-solving and decision-making when working to develop and improve performance	14

Nature and purpose

1

Activity	Individual activity	Team activity
Volleyball		✔
Social dancing		✔
Marathon running	✔	
4 x 400 m relay		✔
Tennis	✔	✔
1500 m	✔	

2 In a directly competitive activity contact between players occurs. For example, in football you can tackle opponents. In indirectly competitive activities your participation is not dependent upon the performance of another performer. Examples of indirectly competitive activities include golf, athletics and trampolining.

3

Activity	Objective/subjective	How results are decided
Gymnastics	subjective	Points at different disciplines such as floor, vault and bar(s)
Netball	objective	More goals scored than the opposition
Cricket	objective	Runs scored/other team bowled out
Table tennis	objective	Number of games won. Each game up to 21 points
Ice dancing	subjective	Marks for technical merit and artistic impression
Swimming	objective	Time taken decides 1st, 2nd, 3rd, etc.

4 Example answers:

Individual activity: Golf
Explanation: Extra holes are played until a winner is found.

Team activity: Football
Explanation: Replays, extra time, 'golden goal' and penalty shoot outs can all be used to decide the winner.

5 Example answer:

Activity: Athletics (track)
Explanation: Running events are decided by judges who have to make a decision about who is the winner. Photo finishes are often needed.

6 Example answer:

Activity: Gymnastics (floor)
Explanation: For a floor sequence, the judges need to consider such factors as the difficulty of different moves, the way the mat area is used and how well the sequence links to the music used.

7 Competitive table tennis and badminton games take place indoors to ensure fairness. Factors such as the weather would make games outside unrealistic. Indoor games are also much more likely to be of better quality than outdoor games of these activities.

8

'I enjoy getting out and meeting other people. We all take part together and then go out afterwards.'	Social
'I like the challenge. I need the thrill of competing against myself when I am rock climbing.'	Personal
'Regular exercise is good for me. It is not too difficult, but demanding enough to help me to live a long and healthy life.'	Health
'Swimming is my favourite sport. The longer events are great for my endurance and the sprint events are great for improving power.'	Physical

9 Each answer should provide a correct identification of type of activity linked to a logical well-described explanation of why you value participation in each of the activities.

10 Example answers:

Younger age activity: Gymnastics
Explanation: You are most likely to participate in gymnastics at a young age only. Gymnastics requires considerable flexibility and a very good power-to-weight ratio. You are most likely to have these physical qualities at a young age.

Lifelong activity: Golf
Explanation: Golf is a skilful game but is not too physically demanding. You can take your time playing. It is therefore a suitable activity for all ages.

11 Example answers:

Activity: Basketball	Factor chosen: Disability
Explanation: Most games halls have wheelchair access. Wheelchair basketball is now a very popular activity. Major events such as the Paralympic Games have helped promote sport for the less able-bodied.	

Activity: Skiing	Factor chosen: Weather
Explanation: The weather can affect your skiing progress. Good weather can help your skiing while poor weather can result in limited snow and often poor overhead conditions.	

12 See example answer provided with question.

13 See example answer provided with question.

14 It makes the winning of the game easier as you are trying to play to your strengths.

15 See example answer provided with question.

16 See example answer provided with question. Other correct answers have to explain the importance of the personal qualities required. Personal qualities include: honesty; fairness; being able to work with others as part of an official team of referees, assistant referees, line judges, timekeepers, etc.

17 See example answer provided with question. Other correct answers have to explain the importance of the physical qualities required in different roles. Other possible physical qualities include different aspects of fitness (cardiorespiratory endurance, muscular endurance, speed, strength, power, flexibility).

18 In football you can signal with your arm where you wish the ball to be played towards. Your team mates can see your signal and play the ball to the intended area.

19 See example answer provided with question.

Official/Formal and unwritten rules

20 See example answer provided with question. Other correct answers have to link the item of equipment selected to safe participation in the chosen activity.

21 See example answer provided with question.

22 See example answer provided with question.

23 See example answer provided with question.

24 See example answer provided with question.

25 Example answer:

Advantage 1: The practice is more likely to be successful because of the extra player/players.
Advantage 2: Attackers are under less pressure than usual. This allows confidence in possession to increase.

Other answers could include the advantages of finding space more easily, of having more opportunities to refine skills and of having more time to carry out specific moves.

26 See example answer provided with question. Answer must be specific to one identified activity throughout.

27 Example answer:

Advantage 1: Each player has a greater chance to be more involved in the game.
Advantage 2: Each player is able to keep up with the game more as the pitch is smaller.

Other answers could include advantages relating to fewer rules, shorter playing time, working more easily with team mates.

Roles and function

28 Example answer:

Activity	Role	Task description
Badminton	Opponent	I played an attacking game based on using smashes and downward shots whenever I could.
Volleyball	Team mate	I set as accurately as I could so that my team mates who were spiking had every chance of winning each rally with their spike.
Basketball	Official	I worked as a timekeeper. When the ball was out of play, I stopped the clock.
Gymnastics	Helper	My partner gave me advice on how to perform my handstand correctly, and then supported me.

29 See example answer provided with question.

30 See example answer provided with question.

31 See example answer provided with question.

Structure and Function

32 (a) **Oxygen transport system**: The main aim of the oxygen transport system is to help you **exercise**. As you **increase** oxygen intake during exercise (by breathing in) you can participate and train in more demanding ways. The lungs, heart, blood and **muscles** all play an important part in the oxygen transport system. The **respiratory** and **circulatory** systems work together to provide muscles with oxygen. This enables you to exercise.

(b) **The circulatory system**: The heart (a muscular pump) is at the centre of the circulatory system. The four chambers of the heart are mostly made up of cardiac muscle. By contracting and relaxing the heart muscles can **pump** blood around the body. The **contractions** of the heart means that blood is pumped around the body in surges which are called the pulse **beat** of the heart. The **arteries** carry blood away from the body to the vital organs and limbs (oxygenated blood) and **veins** return blood to the heart (deoxygenated blood).

(c) **The respiratory system** enables air to be inhaled (breathed in). This allows your circulatory system to work effectively. When you breathe in, oxygen enters your **lungs** and is absorbed into your blood. The **oxygenated** blood allows the cells within your body to use **energy** to help you exercise. As you exercise a **waste** product known as carbon dioxide is produced. This is returned to the lungs by your blood as the circulatory system continues and when you **breathe** out the carbon dioxide leaves your body. When you exercise your breathing is controlled automatically by your brain. You do not often have to 'think' about breathing.

33 Benefit 1: It increases the size of your heart.
Benefit 2: It enables more blood to be pushed around the body following a contraction of your heart muscles.
Benefit 3: It lowers your heart rate

34 Benefit 1: It enables you to measure accurately how much oxygen you can take into your lungs.
Benefit 2: This enables you to compare your maximal oxygen uptake or VO2 max as training progresses. For example, at rest you usually breathe about 12-15 times per minute, but this can increase to 30–40 times per minute when exercising.

35 Reason 1: As lactic acid builds up in your muscles they will become fatigued. This will mean that the muscles cannot work as hard as previously.
Reason 2: Only as a result of slowing down can you breathe frequently and deeply. This pattern of breathing will help you increase your oxygen uptake and begin the process of lactic acid removal.

36 I would plan to train regularly so that my working muscles could get used to the demands of training. This would help delay the build up of lactic acid. This is why in longer running/swimming races it is advisable to start at a modest pace which you can sustain. I would also have a warm down following demanding training. The warm down would allow the effects of any oxygen debt to slowly disappear.

37 Your skeleton has four major functions: it supports your **body**; it protects vital **organs** (heart, lungs); **blood** is produced within longer bones such as the thigh (femur) and it enables **movements** to occur.

38

a	Muscles are attached to the bones of the skeleton by a connective tissue known as a **tendon**.
b	**Ligaments** join bones to other bones and help provide stability in joints by preventing over-stretching and over-twisting.
c	**Cartilage** acts a buffer to protect bones.

39 As one set of leg muscles contracts (the agonist), the opposite set of muscles extends (the antagonist). In this example, the high jumper's front thigh muscles contract (while the back thigh muscles become extended) to straighten the take-off leg and power the jump.

40 (i)

Knee: Hinge
Hip: Ball and socket
Shoulder: Ball and socket
Elbow: Hinge

(ii)   A hinge joint can move in one plane only (opening and closing like a door) whereas a ball and socket joint can move in all planes.

41

Joint used: Knee joint (Hinge)
Explanation: The knee joint allows the upper and lower leg bones to move relative to each other (i.e. the knee bends). The tendons join muscles to bones. As the muscles contract (shorten in length), they pull on the tendons which pull on the bones to produce movement. Then the opposing muscles contract and pull on their tendons to move the bones in the other direction.

42 See example answer provided with question.

Aspects of fitness 1: Physical fitness

43 Your muscles need energy which is supplied by food and **oxygen**. As you breathe in, air enters your **lungs**. There, it is absorbed into your **blood** and pumped round your body by your **heart**.

44 See example answer provided with question.

45 Ensuring that any fitness test for measuring cardiorespiratory endurance is simple and straightforward to complete improves the chances of the test results being accurate. This is because complex skills, which can complicate and lessen the validity of results, are not involved in the test. In addition, simple and straightforward tests should mean that instructions can be clearly understood by those completing the test and by those monitoring test procedures.

46

Benefit 1: The heart becomes bigger and more efficient. More blood can be pushed to the muscles per heart beat (stroke volume).
Benefit 2: More air can be breathed in by the lungs (increased vital capacity). This gives the body more oxygen in each breath.

47 (i)

- I would need to calculate my training zone.
- I would carry out specific training that would raise my pulse rate into my training zone. (Long continuous running would be one option.)
- I would ensure that my pulse stayed within my training zone for between 20–30 minutes for my training to be effective.

(ii)   I would regularly check my pulse to ensure my heart rate was within my training zone.

48 A simple method for measuring your pulse rate when monitoring your cardiorespiratory endurance training is to count your pulse for 6 seconds and multiply your answer by 10 to get your pulse rate per minute. After cardiorespiratory exercise you will probably be able to measure your pulse by placing a hand over you heart or by measuring your pulse rate at the neck.

49 As you exercise, it takes a short time for your heart rate to increase. During this time, your need for oxygen is greater than your supply. You work anaerobically for a while – hence the term 'oxygen debt'.

50 Interval training would work well for developing anaerobic endurance. This is because high effort could be followed by lighter effort which would help your body to remove lactic acid and reduce your oxygen debt.

51 • Cyclists need muscular endurance to keep their leg muscles working for a long time. **Correct**
  • Hockey players need muscular endurance to help them shoot. **False**
  • When kayaking, my arm muscles need muscular endurance when going upstream. **Correct**
  • On the trampoline, you need muscular endurance to complete a 5-bounce sequence. **False**

52 It is necessary to isolate muscle groups when measuring muscular endurance so that you can check on how specific muscle groups are performing. For example, the Bent Knee Sit-Up Test tests for muscular endurance of the stomach (abdominal) muscles. By laying on the floor with hands behind your head, knees bent with feet flat on floor you can isolate the stomach muscles.

53 (i)

Sit-ups: Abdominals	*Dips:* Arms and shoulders
Burpees: Legs, abdominals and shoulders	*Shuttle run:* Legs and shoulders
Press-ups: Arms and shoulders	*Step-ups:* Legs

(ii) Example answers:

Exercise 1: Press-ups
Explanation: I could do more of them in the same time.

Exercise 2: Dips
Explanation: I could pause when my arms are low to the bar each time and hold this position for a few seconds.

Exercise 3: Step-ups
Explanation: I could do the exercise for longer: 40 seconds instead of 30 seconds.

54

Reason 1: To provide you with information about your fitness progress at each exercise station.
Reason 2: The information collected would allow you to make decisions about overloading at each station.

55 See example answer provided with question.

56 • Swimmers need strength to keep swimming for a long time. **False**
  • You need strength in your arms and shoulders to hold a handstand for a few seconds. **Correct**
  • Rugby players need strength to be able to tackle. **Correct**
  • You need strength to putt well in golf. **False**

57 See example answer provided with question.

58 The standing long jump test enables you to complete a straightforward test procedure in order to gain reliable and easily measurable information about your level of explosive strength.

59 For a strength training programme, you need to exercise specific **muscle** groups. You need to ensure that the **workload** of each exercise is high with **low** repetitions. As the training programme progresses, you need to add **overload** to the programme.

60 You would alter the weight used. You would use a different combination of workload to repetition. Muscular endurance would require a high number of repetitions with a low workload, approximately 50% of maximum capacity. Strength would require less repetitions but with a higher workload, approximately 80% of maximum capacity.

61 Isometric training exercises are useful for activities where you may need to hold the muscles tense and still (for example, during handstands and other inverted balances in gymnastics where you have to take your whole weight on your arms).

Isotonic training exercises are useful for activities where you may need to move the working muscles (for example, in butterfly and other swimming strokes, where a regular cycle of the arms is required to move your arms through the water).

62

Activity: Rugby (Goal kicking when taking a penalty)
Explanation: When kicking from distance to try and clear the cross-bar in rugby union, a mix of strength and co-ordination is required. Strength from leg muscles is required and co-ordination helps the kicking action to be fluent which is useful for gaining height and distance in the kick.

63 See example answer provided with question.

64 This means that your test results will link closely to specific needs in hockey.

65 Speed is best improved by increasing **strength** in the main **muscles** required for different activities. When training to improve speed you will be using **anaerobic** (without oxygen) energy most. For this reason you need to ensure that your rest and **recovery** time is long enough. This often means that you would work for 1 repetition of an exercise and rest for 4 times as long.

66 See example answer provided with question.

67 See example answer provided with question.

68 • Swimmers need power for their racing dive at the start of the race. **Correct**
   • You need power to dig the ball successfully in volleyball. **False**
   • Hockey goalkeepers need power to help them stop fast shots. **False**
   • You need power to throw the discus effectively. **Correct**

69 The Vertical Jump Test or the Standing Long Jump Test are accurate for measuring explosive power as both tests have the same aim of testing the explosive power of the same leg muscles. Both tests are also equally simple to complete.

70 Explosive power is best improved by increasing **strength** in the main **muscles** used for different activities and by completing exercises requiring **speed**. If you are using weight training to improve strength, ensure you take into account your own **weight** when calculating training **values**.

71 To monitor power training effectively requires that training matches the demands of the activity or event as closely as possible. For example, if a long jump competition in athletics is made up of six jumps with each jump separated by a few minutes rest and recovery, it makes sense for effective training to involve a similar number of jumps with similar rest and recovery times.

72 See example answer provided with question.

73 Example answer:

Activity: Tennis	Skill: Service reception
Explanation: The performer has to react quickly to the speed and angle of the serve. Often the chosen return of serve will involve quick court movement to play a powerful return.	

74

Activity	Static or dynamic flexibility?	Where flexibility is most required
Gymnastics – Headstand	Static	The gymnast requires flexibility in the leg muscles to ensure that the legs are extended with pointed toes.
Swimming	Dynamic	The swimmer requires flexibility in their arms and back at the start of their backstroke swimming. Once settled into the swimming stroke, the wide range of movement created by arm and back flexibility helps propulsion, and good leg flexibility ensures streamlining.
Hockey	Dynamic	The hockey player has good knee, hip and back flexibility. This enables them to get low to the ground and behind the ball before passing the ball.
Rugby	Static	Forwards in rugby try in certain scrums to hold the scrum steady. They are trying to use their static strength to prevent the other team's forwards from driving them backwards.
Athletics	Dynamic	The triple jumper has good flexibility in all major joints – knee, hip, back and shoulder. This enables them to carry speed forward throughout the different phases of the triple jump.

75 It is important to extend and stretch carefully so that you do not injure yourself through straining muscles. This can often occur if you extend too quickly in a jerky rather than smooth way.

76

Exercise	Static or active?	Aim of exercise
Side-splits	Static	The muscles of the inner thigh and hips are stretched as you gradually move your trunk further forward by carefully extending your fingers and hands. The benefits of the exercise are increased by extending and pointing the toes and by keeping your head low to the ground.
Leg-stretch	Static	The muscles of the back of the thigh (hamstrings) are stretched. By holding your toes and gently pulling against them with your hands you can add to the stretching involved in a controlled way.
Side-stretch	Active	The side muscles of the trunk are stretched by reaching over your head with an extended arm. You can add to the stretching involved by gently reaching further over with the arm and returning to centre and repeating this action a few times before switching to stretching the opposite side. It is important to retain a tall (vertical) posture when completing this active flexibility exercise.

77 The main criteria for monitoring the effectiveness of flexibility training would be to measure the range of movement involved in different actions and to measure whether this was improving or not. It would be possible to complete such monitoring of flexibility through completing a specific fitness test or by evaluating flexibility improvements as part of overall performance, for example, in a game.

78 See example answer provided with question.

79 To make stretching movements for defending in volleyball, I needed **flexibility**.
To be able to throw the javelin far, I needed **power**.
To rebound continuously during the whole game, I needed **muscular endurance**.
To make short fast runs into the penalty area, I needed **speed**.
To keep going for the full 90 minutes, I needed **cardiorespiratory endurance**.
To hold a handstand, I needed **strength**.

80 The midfield players in our team needed **cardiorespiratory endurance** as they had to do so much running in the game. In defence, the defenders needed **speed** to cover for each other against attacking players. In attack, our attackers needed **strength** to keep possession of the ball when under pressure from defenders challenging them. They also needed **power** when shooting. The goalkeeper needed **flexibility** when diving to save shots. All players needed some **muscular endurance** in their arm and leg muscles.

Aspects of fitness 2: Skill-related fitness

81 Co-ordination is the ability to control movements **smoothly** and **fluently**. To perform in a co-ordinated way, groups of muscles work in a specific **sequence** to create effective movements. For difficult skills with **complex** co-ordination requirements specific practices are required. A triple jumper in athletics practises carrying speed through to the final jump **phase**. This requires co-ordinated body movements in each phase of the jump. Effective co-ordination should ensure that there is no **jerkiness** when performing a triple jump.

82 See example answer provided with question.

83 When dribbling in hockey you need to be able to run fast and adjust your body shape to maintain control of the stick and the ball. Good agility helps you do this by enabling you to move your body quickly and precisely.

84 See example answer provided with question.

85

Balance	Static or dynamic?	Aim of balance
Dancers	Static	The dancers require to hold a static stable balance once in position.
Rock climber	Dynamic	The rock climber requires to stay in dynamic balance as they climb. Movements require to link together so that balance is retained.
Discus thrower	Dynamic	The discus thrower requires to stay in balance as they turn and generate power before releasing the discus.

86 See example answer provided with question.

87 Example answers:

Individual activity: Swimming
Explanation: Reacting quickly to the start signal enables you to begin your dive start and get into your swimming stroke as quickly as possible.

Team activity: Rugby
Explanation: When the referee starts and restarts play from the centre line the forwards must react quickly to the kick, so that they can either win possession of the ball or put pressure on the opposing team as soon as possible.

88 See example answer provided with question.

Aspects of fitness 3: Mental fitness

89 Example answer:

In orienteering you are often running and thinking for a long time, possibly up to one hour. You need to anticipate this before you start. This means that you can begin running at a pace you can sustain for the whole time. This will help you think more clearly as you navigate your route and make difficult route selection decisions.

90 See example answer provided with question.

Training and its effects

91 A warm up is an important part of your **preparation** for activity. It should begin with some gentle **jogging** to raise your **pulse**. After this, you should do some **stretching** exercises that will help your flexibility. You may then want to practise some of the **skills** involved in the activity.

92 See example answer provided with question. Your answer should include details of two specific exercises you used.

93 (i)   To raise the pulse and increase blood flow to the muscles.

(ii) To allow muscles to move more easily and to improve the flexibility in joints.

(iii) It reduces stiffness in muscles and helps return the body to a resting state.

94

Physical fitness training programme	→	Specificity	→	Progressive Overload	→	Frequency
						Duration
						Intensity

95 (i)   It allows you to set an appropriate workload. It is also easy to measure improvements to your fitness.

(ii) Overload can be added in three ways. Each exercise can be made more difficult (intensity), each exercise can be performed more often (frequency) and each exercise can be performed for longer (duration).

96 Duration refers to the length of planned time spent training. The **duration** of your training varies according to the **demands** of the activity. Within the context of a training programme short, **intensive** training sessions promote **anaerobic** fitness improvement; longer, moderately intensive sessions develop **aerobic** endurance.

97 Over training can be avoided by carefully calculating the appropriate work and rest and recovery times. Careful pulse monitoring and measuring your fitness at the beginning of a training period are two important steps for helping you avoid over training. In energetic anaerobic based training it is beneficial for the pulse to return to a resting level between sets to avoid over exertion. Over training can also be avoided by adapting the levels of frequency, intensity and duration within your training.

98 See example answer provided with question.

99 Lactate tolerance training is beneficial for many activities which last around 60–90 minutes. In such activities a high level of overall aerobic activity is required with some shorter periods of anaerobic activity included. For such activities it is useful to get used to the oxygen debt which can build up in muscles. For this reason lactate tolerance training is useful.

100 When you stop training your body reverts to the condition it was in before you began training. The time this takes to happen will be dependent upon how long you trained for. If your training has been short then the training benefits will only last for a few weeks before reversibility occurs. If you have trained for a longer period it takes a longer time before regression occurs.

101 Each explanation should refer to applying the principle of progressive overload by making the exercise more demanding (intensity), carried out for longer (duration) or carried out more often (frequency).

102 It enables high **intensity** training to be undertaken. Such training links to periods of rest to avoid **fatigue** occurring.

It has the capacity to be useful for both **aerobic** and **anaerobic** purposes.

Progressive **overload** can be carefully added to your training.

103 **method of training** The answers for both the individual activity and the team activity chosen need to show a relevant and correctly explained relationship between the activity, aspect of fitness and method of training chosen.

fitness test The answers for both the individual activity and the team activity chosen need to show a relevant and correctly explained relationship between the activity, aspect of fitness and fitness test chosen.

104 It can develop physical, skill-related and mental aspects of fitness at the same time.

It is specific to the activity being followed.

Techniques

105 When learning to perform a new skill or technique, you try to make it as **easy** as possible. You can do this by making the **movements** flow together in a simple order. As you become better, you can make the skill or technique more **complex**. You can make your skill or technique practice more **difficult** in many ways, for example, by practising for longer. This may make it more **tiring** for you.

106 The correct order is: (1) run-up (2) take-off (3) first flight (4) second flight (5) landing.

107

Activity	Gymnastics	Badminton	Basketball
Skill/technique	Forward roll	High serve	Jump shot
Preparation 1	Feet together	Stand 'side on'	Feet together
Preparation 2	Head tucked in	Take racket back	Look at target
Action 1	Take weight on hands	Transfer weight forward	Controlled jump
Action 2	Keep legs together	Smooth racket swing	Release at full height
Recovery 1	Open out carefully	High follow-through	Land in balance
Recovery 2	Finish standing still	Be ready for next shot	React to shot result

108 See example answer provided with question.

109 See example answer provided with question.

110 It is useful for establishing your own strengths and weaknesses.

It helps you decide on your practices priorities.

111 See example answer provided with question.

112 See example answer provided with question.

3 SKILLS AND TECHNIQUES

113

Activity: Swimming	
Technique: Back crawl	
Push off from the side, gentle continuous leg kick, take six arm strokes, then stand.	3
Push off from the side, hold one float under each arm, leg kick for one width.	1
Push off from the side, swim continuously for one 20 m length of back crawl, full stroke.	4
Push off from the side, hold one float across chest, leg kick for one length of the pool.	2

114 Example answers:

Reason 1: You have more time to practise different skills and techniques you have learned.
Reason 2: You have more confidence to try different moves.
Reason 3: You can practise under less pressure as there are fewer defenders.

Ways of developing skill

115 When planning practices you should ensure that practice is safe and matches your level of ability. For example, in gymnastics you need to carefully estimate whether you have the ability to complete new techniques. In addition, you need to ensure that the gymnastics area is set out safely and that you have completed a suitable warm up and will conclude the practice session with a warm down.

116 (i) You can become familiar with the movements involved in a skill or technique. The movements can become automatic.

(ii) You might become tired. You can become bored by repeating the same practice.

117 • Make the defender play 'active' rather than 'passive' defence.

• Make it 3 v 1 instead of 4 v 1 – this will make the three players work harder.

• Make the four attackers play 'two-touch' then, later, 'one-touch' only. This will make ball control and possession more difficult to achieve.

118 Sometimes it is difficult to break down continuous actions such as a gymnastics vault into whole-part-whole sections. It is easier to practise such a skill by building the skill up progressively, adding to the difficulty of the vault bit by bit.

119 • You can concentrate more on other parts of the game. For example, in basketball, being able to dribble correctly means that you can look up and see who is open to receive a pass.

• You can move more easily while still paying attention to other things. For example, in badminton, you can move backwards and get into a side-on position to play an overhead clear shot. Avoiding looking down makes it easier to keep looking at the shuttlecock.

120 See example answer provided with question.

121 A principle of **effective** practice is that you train for a suitable training time. Too short and improvements will be limited. Too long and you may become **fatigued** and prone to picking up an injury. Training for too long a time can also lead to **boredom** and a gradual reduction in the amount of progress you make. Having **varied** practices is one effective way of reducing boredom.

122 The work-to-rest ratio takes into account:
- your previous **experience** in an activity
- your level of **practical** ability
- the **difficulty** of the skill involved
- the **physical** demands involved in the practice.

123 (i) See example answer provided with question.

(ii) See example answer provided with question.

124
- Receiving feedback immediately after your performance is best. **True**
- Negative feedback about what you are doing wrong will help you learn. **False**
- Knowledge of results is a useful form of external feedback. **True**
- Detailed feedback on at least 10 different points is needed to learn simple skills. **False**
- Positive feedback on a few key points works well. **True**
- You receive internal feedback during your performance. **True**

125 Answers could include the following points:
- Feedback should be positive, clear and precise.
- He should give feedback as soon as possible after performance.
- He should focus on a few key points that will help the performer.

126 Internal feedback is the feedback you 'feel' yourself during your performance. For example, when swimming, you can 'feel' whether your hand is in the right 'catch' position before the pull begins. External feedback either comes from other people (for example, your coach discusses the qualities in your performance) or from the results of your performance, both during and after activity (for example, race times).

127 See example answer provided with question.

128 A partner can help record information about your performance, for example by completing an observation schedule.

A partner can practise against you as you develop different skills and techniques. They can adjust the level of opposition in practice, sometimes providing passive opposition, sometimes active opposition.

A partner can be useful as a critical friend for talking to you about your performance targets.

Mechanical principles

129 The gymnast performing the headstand has a static centre of gravity as she is trying to hold her balance above her base of support (which is created by her arms and head). The skier has a dynamic (constantly moving) centre of gravity as she is moving when skiing. In this example, the skier's centre of gravity is affected by the turning of the skis and the terrain.

130 See example answer provided with question.

131 See example answers provided with question.

132 A swimmer uses **force** to overcome **resistance**. A rugby union player taking a penalty kick from a long **distance** has a long follow-through in her kick. This helps add **power** to the kick. A long distance runner keeps his centre of **gravity** at the same **height** as he runs forward.

133 See example answer provided with question.

134 See example answer provided with question.

135 See example answers provided with question.

136 Example answer:

In swimming front crawl the rotation of the shoulder joint enables the arm to pull and recover with little loss of streamlining to the body. Turning the upper body slightly helps the shoulder joint to rotate and perform the action.

137 See example answer provided with question.

138 (i) See example answer provided with question.

(ii) See example answer provided with question.

139 In throwing the javelin in athletics a good follow through enables you to pull the throwing arm forward as quickly and powerfully as possible, realising that as you complete your throw you can regain balance on your new lead foot. To allow some distance for the follow through to occur, you should ensure that you begin the action part of the throw some metres back from the line from where throws are measured.

140 (i) Gymnastics – forward roll

Preparation: Low start position, balanced, knees flexed, facing forward.
Action: Controlled medium speed, drive from knees controlling speed of roll, slightly open tuck, rounded back, legs together. First hands then upper to lower back roll on the ground before beginning recovery.
Recovery: Use medium speed of roll to regain standing position, feet slightly apart to regain balance.

(ii) Basketball – left handed lay-up

Preparation: Face towards basket, balanced, flexed posture.
Action: Run towards basket, take off right foot and jump as high as possible laying the ball gently onto the backboard.
Recovery: Land both feet together at the same time in balanced, flexed posture.

(iii) Tennis – backhand

Preparation: Run towards ball. Move into 'side-on' position as early as possible and take racquet back in preparation for action phase. Watch speed and direction of ball closely. Upper body turns away from approaching ball, legs bent.
Action: Fast powerful striking action, shoulders unwind when striking ball, transfer weight from back to front foot.
Recovery: Complete follow through and regain balanced alert posture with racquet held in front of body, ready to move and prepare for next shot.

(iv) Gymnastics – handspring

Preparation: Extended position in run-up approach, smooth controlled accelerating running action.
Action: Legs bend to begin drive, arms reaching out, extended and together. Both hands strike mat together. Fast strong legs swing to generate rotation. Legs keep extended as they overtake arms.
Recovery: Legs land together when resuming standing position, arms used to help regain balance as necessary.

(v) Gymnastics – neck spring

Preparation: Extended position in run-up approach, smooth controlled accelerating running action.
Action: Two-footed take-off. Controlled flight onto box top. Reach out with arms which make contact with the box top together. Shoulders lowered to box top, arms bend to allow rounded shape before drive to produce open arched extended position to create flight off box top.
Recovery: Legs land together when resuming standing position, arms used to help regain balance as necessary.

141 Through shared discussion with your classmates and teacher, you should work towards producing agreed answers*, which are of similar quality to those shown above for question 140.

*Please note that these answers are full, clear and detailed. You should attempt to write answers of similar quality when preparing for your examination.